CHLOE and her BAD BOWS

Written by Melissa Muken

Drawings by Anjelika Rijvers

CHLOE and her BAZILLION BOWS

Written by Melissa Muken   Drawings by Anjelika Rijvers

To my loving family. I thank you a bazillion times over.

ISBN: 9781698531991

One bow

Two bows

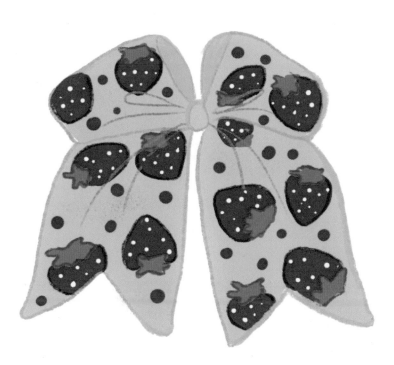

Three bows

Four

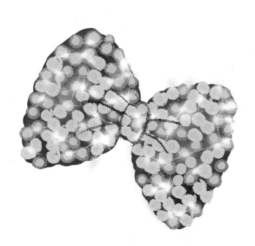

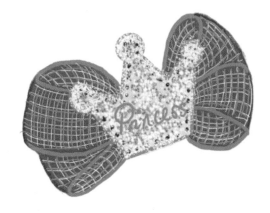

I have a thousand on my floor.

I sometimes wear them in my hair.

Or on my reading chair.

I also wear them to school.

They even look great in the pool!

I wear them to a Broadway show.

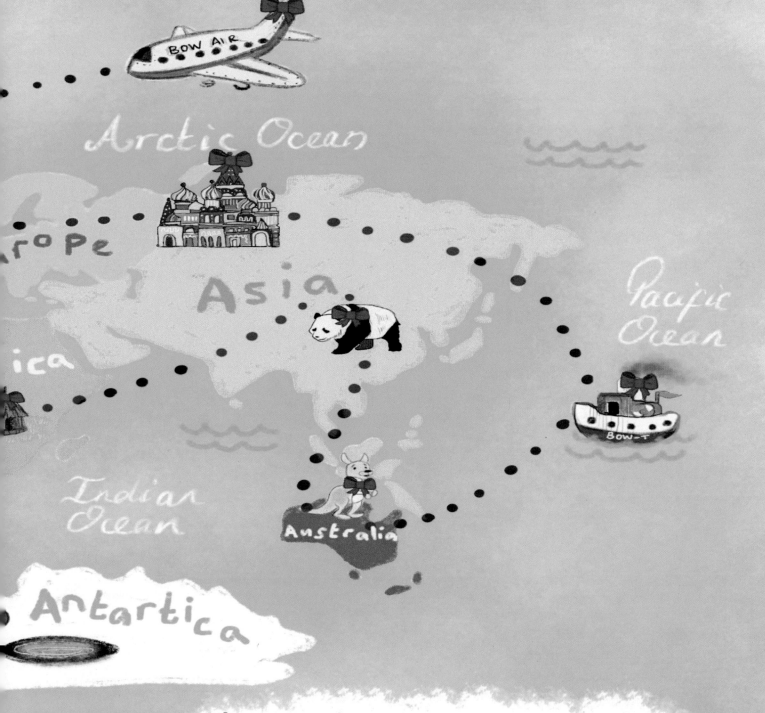

I wear them everywhere I go!

I just want rows and rows of lovely,
colorful, shiny bows.

If I am good and do my chores,
I get a bow as a reward.

I have green

pink

and orange too.

Some have patterns

some are blue.

Some have stripes.

Some have dots.

My favorite has glitter with purple spots!

Some are **BIG.**

 Some are small.

Although they are different,
I love them all!

I am tough and strong
and play sports too... all while wearing
a bow or two!

One bow

Two bows

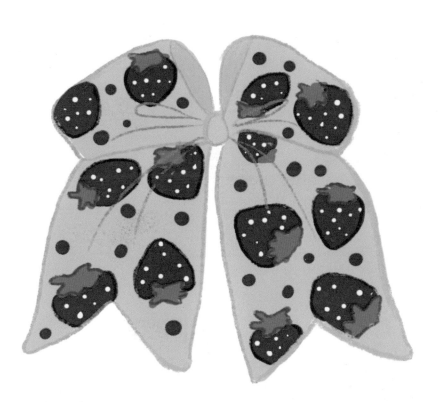

Three bows

Four

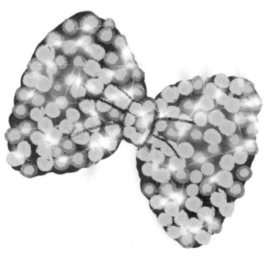

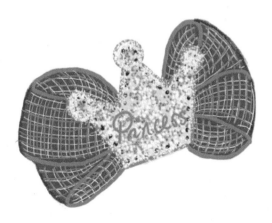

I wish I had a **BAZILLION** more!!!

Made in United States
Orlando, FL
10 February 2022